The Universe

The Planets

Anne Welsbacher
ABDO & Daughters

Published by Abdo & Daughters, 4940 Viking Drive, Suite 622, Edina, Minnesota 55435.

Copyright © 1997 by Abdo Consulting Group, Inc., Pentagon Tower, P.O. Box 36036, Minneapolis, Minnesota 55435 USA. International copyrights reserved in all countries. No part of this book may be reproduced in any form without written permission from the publisher.

Printed in the United States.

Cover and Interior Photo credits: Peter Arnold, Inc.
Archive Photos
Wide World Photos
Illustrations: Tim Blough
Edited by Bob Italia

Library of Congress Cataloging-in-Publication Data

Welsbacher, Anne, 1955-
The planets / Anne Welsbacher.
p. cm. — (The universe)
Includes index.
Summary: A simple description of the nine planets that make up our solar system.
ISBN 1-56239-718-4
    1. Planets—Juvenile literature.   [1. Planets.] I. Title. II . Series: Welsbacher, Anne, 1955-
Universe.
  QB602.W45 1997
  523.4—dc20   96-18862
                                                                      CIP
                                                                       AC

ABOUT THE AUTHOR
Anne Welsbacher is the director of publications for the Science Museum of Minnesota. She has written and edited science books and articles for children, and has written for national and regional publications on science, the environment, the arts, and other topics.

Contents

The Planets

Nine planets **orbit** the Sun. They are Mercury, Venus, Earth, Mars, Jupiter, Saturn, Neptune, Uranus, and Pluto.

While orbiting, each planet spins like a top on its **axis.** Smaller objects called **satellites** spin around some of the planets. The planets, their satellites, and the Sun make up our **Solar System**.

Opposite page: Six of the planets in our Solar System. The Earth is seen over the horizon of the Moon, with a Sun flare on the edge of the Earth.

Mercury

Mercury (MIRK-yer-ee) is the closest planet to the Sun. It is also the second smallest planet in the **Solar System**. The side of Mercury that faces the Sun is very hot.

Mercury has **craters**, small hills, and flat areas. Much of the planet is made of **iron** and **nickel**. Mercury's north pole has ice.

Mercury also has a strange **orbit**. It spins slowly on its **axis**. But it orbits quickly around the Sun.

Opposite page:
Illustration of the planet Mercury.

Venus

Venus (VEE-nus) is the second planet from the Sun. It is the brightest object in the night sky, except for the Moon. It is almost the same size as Earth.

Venus is so hot that lead would melt on its surface. A thick coat of clouds traps the Sun's heat close to the planet. This is called the **greenhouse effect**.

Venus has many large **craters**. Venus also has volcanoes. Some of them might be active.

Venus seen from Mariner 10, 450,000 miles (724,000 km) away.

Opposite page: Computer generated 3-D view of Venus' surface.

Earth

Earth is the third planet from the Sun. It has two things no other planets have: life and oceans.

Earth is tilted on its **axis**. The tilt causes the four seasons: spring, summer, fall, and winter.

Earth has a hot, active **core**, which causes the surface to move. This movement forms volcanoes and causes earthquakes.

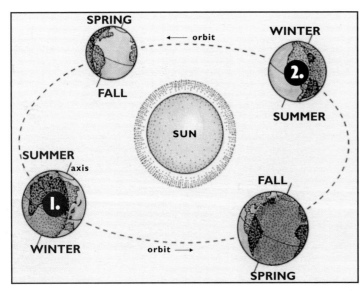

When the northern part of the Earth tilts toward the Sun (1.), it is summer in the north. At the same time, the southern part tilts away from the Sun, where it is winter in the south. When the northern part of the Earth tilts away from the Sun (2.), it is winter in the north. At the same time, the southern part tilts toward the Sun, where it is summer in the south.

A view of Earth from the Moon.

Mars

Mars (MARZ) is the fourth planet from the Sun. It is the third-smallest planet, about half the size of Earth. It has two tiny moons.

Mars is called the red planet because there is rust in its soil. Mars has volcanoes. One of them, Olympus Mons, is the largest volcano in the **Solar System.**

Like Earth, Mars is tilted on its **axis**. The planet is hotter in some seasons than in others. Mars also has an **atmosphere** and winds.

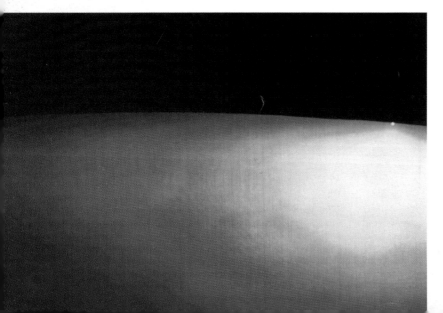

Sunrise on Mars.

A view of Mars from the Viking orbiter.

Jupiter

Jupiter (JOOP-ih-ter) is the fifth planet from the Sun. It is also the largest planet—bigger than all the other planets put together!

Jupiter has a huge spot on its surface called the Great Red Spot. This spot is a giant storm that is two times larger than Earth. The storm is always moving.

Jupiter is made of gases and clouds. The planet gives off heat, like the Sun. It also has 16 moons.

Opposite page: Jupiter is the largest planet in our Solar System. The big red spot on the bottom left is a storm twice the size of Earth.

Saturn

Saturn (SAT-ern) is the second-largest planet. It is made up of gases and clouds. Like Jupiter, Saturn gives off heat.

Saturn has thousands of rings around it. The rings have many colors and sizes. They are made of ice and rock.

Saturn has 20 or more moons—more than any other planet. Some, called **shepherd moons**, might hold the rings in place.

Saturn's ring system seen from Voyager 2.

Saturn.

Uranus

Uranus (YER-an-us) is the third-largest planet. It is made of gases and clouds that give it a blue-green color. Under its clouds, Uranus might have water.

Uranus is tipped on its side. It may have been hit by a large **comet** speeding through space.

Uranus has 15 moons and thin rings. Some of these rings are so thin they are almost invisible. Scientists think the rings are still being formed today.

Opposite page: Voyager 2 on its approach to Uranus. Notice the thin rings circling the planet.

Neptune

Neptune (NEP-toon) is the second-farthest planet from the Sun. It is bluish colored and made of gases.

Though it is far from the Sun, Neptune is not very cold. It might make its own heat, like Jupiter and Saturn.

Neptune spins very fast on its **axis**, and has eight moons. One of these moons **orbits** backward around Neptune!

A filtered image of Neptune taken by Voyager 2.

Pluto

Pluto (PLEW-toe) is the farthest planet from the Sun. It was discovered in 1930.

Pluto is also the smallest planet. It is made mostly of gas. It has one moon, Charon, discovered in 1978.

Pluto has a wide **orbit** around the Sun. Sometimes its orbit brings it inside Neptune's orbit.

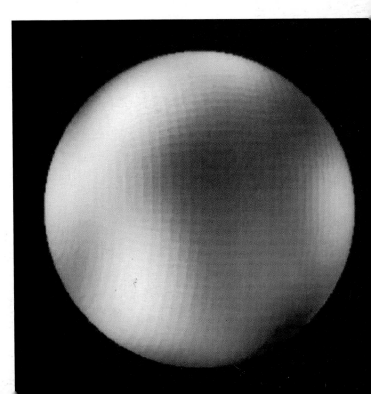

Computer-enhanced photo of Pluto taken from the Hubble Space Telescope.

Planet Facts

Largest planet .... Jupiter (88,700 miles, 142,700 km across)

Smallest planet .... Pluto (1,420 miles, 2,285 km across)

Planet with most moons .... Saturn (23 or more)

Planet with most rings .... Saturn (thousands)

Planet closest to the Sun .... Mercury (36 million miles, 57.9 million km)

Planet farthest from the Sun .... Pluto (3.66 billion miles, 5.89 billion km)

Hottest planet .... Venus (850 F, 455 C)

Coldest planet .... Pluto (-400 F, -240 C)

Planet with the fastest orbit .... Mercury (30 miles, 48 km per second)

Glossary

atmosphere (AT-muss-fear)—the air that surrounds the Earth.

axis—the imaginary line down the middle of a planet; a planet spins around its axis.

comet—a heavenly body that looks like a star with a cloudy tail of light.

core—the center of a planet.

crater—a hole in the ground shaped like a bowl.

greenhouse effect—a condition in which heat is trapped close to a planet's surface by a thick coat of clouds.

iron—the most common metal, from which steel is made.

nickel—a hard, silvery-white metal.

orbit—the circle-shaped journey that each planet travels around the Sun.

satellites (SAT-uh-lites)—objects that spin around planets. Moons and rings are satellites.

shepherd (SHEP-erd) **moons**—moons that keep rings in place around their planets, named for shepherds who keep sheep from wandering away.

Solar System—the Sun, the nine planets, and the moons and rings of the planets.

Index